You Got This!

100 Tips for Being
Your Stress-Free Best

Helaine Becker

Scholastic Canada Ltd.
Toronto New York London Auckland Sydney
Mexico City New Delhi Hong Kong Buenos Aires

Scholastic Canada Ltd.
604 King Street West, Toronto, Ontario M5V 1E1, Canada

Scholastic Inc.
557 Broadway, New York, NY 10012, USA

Scholastic Australia Pty Limited
PO Box 579, Gosford, NSW 2250, Australia

Scholastic New Zealand Limited
Private Bag 94407, Botany, Manukau 2163, New Zealand

Scholastic Children's Books
Euston House, 24 Eversholt Street, London NW1 1DB, UK

www.scholastic.ca

Library and Archives Canada Cataloguing in Publication

Title: You got this! : 100 tips for being your stress-free best / Helaine Becker.

Names: Becker, Helaine, author.

Identifiers: Canadiana 20190084405 | ISBN 9781443170451 (softcover)

Subjects: LCSH: Stress management for children—Juvenile literature. | LCSH: Stress management—

Juvenile literature. | LCSH: Stress in children—Juvenile literature.

Classification: LCC BF723.S75 B43 2019 | DDC j155.4/189042—dc23

Photos © Dreamstime: Ienchik, Aerial3, Alena Ohneva, Anatolyi Deryenko, Andrey
Kozhekin, Andrey Roussanov, Andrey Yanushkov, Anna Vynohradova, Antart,
Artishokcs , Artyway, Azat Gaisin, Beaniebeagle, Blue67, Burin Suporntawesuk,
Carlacpdesign, Claudiu Badea, Dannyphoto80, Daria Karuna, Dg Studio, Evgeniya
Mokeeva, Fajar Pramudianto, Fenix84, Freud, Gstudioimagen, Ilonai, Irina Kuzevanova,
Irinakrivoruchko, Isabel Poulin, Jarenwicklund, Jozef Micic, Julia Titova, Kannaa,
Katerina Chumakova, Katsiaryna Kulikova, Lindybugdesign, Nmarques74, Olesia
Agudova, Ondřej Kulíšek, Oxanaart, Pavlo I, Photosaurus, Prairat Fhunta, Spelagranda,
Studiconco, Tatiana Gavrish, Tupungato, Volha Sharhayeva.

6 5 4 3 2 1   Printed in Canada   121   19 20 21 22 23

MIX
Paper from
responsible sources
FSC® C004071

Table of Contents

Introduction

Life can be so serious . . . serious *fun* that is! All it takes is a little know-how.

In this book, you'll find dozens of ideas and tips for bringing more laughs and adventure into your life. It includes tons of try-it-now suggestions for filling buckets of fun every day.

This book also includes plenty of hard-headed advice for how to reach your goals and make your dreams come true: oodles of energy boosters, social-skill enhancers, confidence builders and task managers you can dip into any time. Whatever comes your way, you've got it covered.

So open your mind (p. 27), mix it up and try something new (p. 11). You'll be taking the first step (p. 73) toward the best you ever.

Add Music and Stir

Music is a powerful mood-changer. A finger-snapping beat, a catchy chorus or a peppy melody can bring a joyful vibe to any situation.

Tidying up your room? Do it to the sound of your favourite hip-hop artist. Got homework? Something soothing and serene playing softly in the background might be the A+ choice.

Sharing your favourite tunes with others is also a great way to bring friends, both new and old, together. Karaoke night, anyone?

So pump up the volume and get out the tambourine.

Music Rocks!

Put Fun on the Calendar

Fun doesn't just appear at your door. You have to plan for it and make it happen!

Start with a fun idea: *I want to have a slumber party with my three besties.* Or *I wonder if I could build the world's tallest house of cards . . .*

Then ask yourself, *Is it doable?* If the answer is yes, that's where the calendar comes in. *Someday* never comes. But *Tuesday at 3* will be here before you know it.

So choose a date and mark it on your schedule — in ink! Organize your supplies and make all your arrangements *now*. By the time that big day arrives, you'll be ready!

When in Doubt, Crowdsource!

Oh no! You can't figure out the answer to that tricky word problem or how to fix the flat tire on your bicycle. You're stumped and feeling defeated. Don't fret. Crowdsource!

Of course you should try to sort things out for yourself first — that builds resilience and stick-to-it-iveness. But when you're stuck and can't find a solution to a problem on your own, a brainstorming session with pals or family members might turn up the exact answer you're looking for. Maybe your peeps will show you a strategy you can use next time to solve the problem on your own.

It's okay to ask for help. Experts don't get to be experts all by their lonesome. Everybody needs a helping hand sometimes.

DON'T Ask for Help

Asking for advice or assistance from others is often a great idea. It can save you time and make your life easier. But there are times when it's better to solve a problem yourself.

Sometimes when you take a shortcut you are really shortchanging yourself. By not doing the work, you lose the chance to learn something deeply, from the inside out.

Solving problems on your own builds confidence; it teaches you that you can rely on yourself in a tough spot. It also builds perseverance, which means you can stick with a difficult task for longer periods of time. That, in turn, leads to mastery and success.

> "The 'silly' question is the first intimation of some totally new development."
>
> – Alfred North Whitehead

Be Curious

Achieving success isn't about having all the right answers. It's about asking the right questions. Knowledge starts with curiosity. So be curious!

Ask questions all the time and take very little for granted. Let the ordinary events of everyday life trigger your curiosity. (What is toothpaste made of, anyway?)

The more questions you have and seek to answer, the more you'll learn. The more you learn, the more capable — and interesting — you will be.

Mix It Up

Do different things. The more variety, the better.
Doing the same things over and over, even if
you enjoy them, is less fun than if you mix it up.

So try something new! Variety is the spice of
life.

Grow a Growth Mindset

Some people believe they are born with certain talents and abilities, and nothing they do will change that. This way of thinking is called a "fixed mindset." Others believe you can develop skills of all kinds through hard work. This way of thinking is called a "growth mindset."

A growth mindset can help you reach your goals. It makes you more likely to work at tasks and be more open to input from others than a fixed mindset does. And those traits are the ones that really work!

If you tend to have a fixed mindset, you're not stuck with it. You can change it. Growing a growth mindset is only a matter of practice. That's what the growth mindset is about, after all!

Put That Growth Mindset to Work!

When faced with new challenges, resist the impulse to say, "I don't have what it takes." Instead, nourish your dreams with these growth-mindset go-tos.

★ Embrace each new challenge with the view that you will learn from it.

★ See failures as temporary setbacks. Catch your breath and try again.

★ Did someone criticize you or your work? Don't turn it into an "always" or "never" statement in your mind, ("I'm not good at washing dishes.") Instead, see it as a guide for improvement. Next time, you'll take more care and do a bang-up job, right?

An Object in Motion Stays in Motion

The alarm rings. You want to cry out, "Nooo! Just one more minute . . ." then hit the snooze button.

Instead, get up and get moving! Once you're in motion, it's easier to stay in motion. You waste less time and accomplish way more. This is one of the most powerful secrets to success. It's so profound it's actually a law — of physics!

Sir Isaac Newton's First Law of Motion states, in part, that an object in motion stays in motion, unless something interferes with that motion. Similarly, if you're at rest — not doing much of anything — you're more likely to remain at rest. You'll be pretty hard to shift too.

So if you want to be the kind of person who gets things done, get moving!

Get extra oomph from this move by connecting with your breath. Inhale when you twist to the right. Exhale when you twist to the left.

Spaghetti Arms

When you find you've been sitting in one place for too long or you feel a bit tight and stressed, it's time to shake it off with this fun and funny move.

1. Stand with your feet hip width apart. Let your arms dangle at your sides, nice and loose like strands of cooked spaghetti.

2. Gently twist at the waist and let your arms swing as you turn.

3. Twist in the other direction. Let your loose, floppy noodle arms swing in the opposite direction along with you.

4. Twist back and forth, back and forth, letting your spaghetti arms swing. Doesn't that feel good?

5. Stop swinging after about ten twists and take a moment to enjoy the sensation of stillness.

Be a Warrior

Yoga is an ancient practice that uses set poses to strengthen the body and the mind. This pose, called Warrior 2, increases both physical and mental stamina.

Here's how to do it:

1. Stand with feet together, arms hanging at your sides. Inhale.

2. Exhale. Step your right foot to the right.

3. Turn your right foot 90 degrees so it points right.

4. Turn your left foot 45 degrees so it also points (partway) to the right.

5. Bend your right knee.

6. Raise your arms parallel to the floor and in line with your legs. Look right above your right hand.

7. Hold the pose. Feel strength flowing through you.

8. Return to standing position. Repeat steps two to seven, this time facing to the left.

Honour Your Breath

Your breath connects your body, your mind and your spirit. Close your eyes and listen to it. Does it sound like waves lapping on a shore?

Like the ocean, your breath is a source of natural power. You tap into that power when you pay attention to the ins and outs, the ebbs and flows, of your own breath.

Your breath is always with you. Let it ground you and energize you.

The Game of Life

Life is full of boring tasks . . . or is it? Everyday routines are daily opportunities for fun.

Try some of these *Risk*-free ideas — you won't be *Sorry!*

- ★ Countdown Challenge! Race against the clock while making your bed.

- ★ Play some garbage-bin basketball with your sister when you take out the trash.

- ★ Quiz a friend for a spelling test in TV game show style. Put on a game show host persona for extra giggles.

You can't always change your situation, but you can change how you approach it. Bring the spirit of play to your day and you're sure to win at the game of life.

Be Spontaneous

"Make a plan and stick to it" is great advice — most of the time. But sometimes a golden opportunity appears out of the blue. When it does, be ready to grab it, even if that means crumpling up your detailed plan.

Being spontaneous — seizing the moment — can bring great joy into your life.

Wag

Dogs live in the moment. They make the most of every second and enjoy each one to the fullest.

So be a dog!

Wag your tail.

Howl at the moon.

Enjoy today.

Ditch the Phone

Our phones have a lot to offer: instant information, a way to stay in touch with friends and family, cat memes — lots of cat memes. But phones have a downside too. They interfere with your ability to stay fully immersed in the here and now. And that's where your life actually happens, not on the tiny screen.

Research shows that people who spend a lot of time on their phones, especially if they use social media, are less happy than people who don't.

So who are the happiest people? The ones who hang out with their friends IRL.

Turn off Other Screens Too

Screens are fun while you're immersed in them. But as soon as you surface, you discover time has passed, the world has moved on, and you've got nothing to show for the time you spent logged on.

Cell phones are probably the worst offenders when it comes to time wastage, but other devices with screens — computers, TVs, video games — are also trouble. They charm you and reel you in, and before you know it, hours have disappeared.

So turn off the screens and live your totally awesome life.

Label It!

Your day is full of many experiences and so many emotions that it can sometimes feel confusing and overwhelming. One way to get a handle on all those swirling feelings is to name them.

Here's how:

1. When a strong emotion washes over you, don't try to push it away. Recognize and acknowledge it.

2. Ask yourself which word best describes the emotion you are feeling.

3. Accept the feeling.

This simple process helps lessen negative feelings and gives you a chance to control them and your behaviour in more positive ways. You'll be less likely to snap at your dad when he asks you to set the table, or fly into a rage when you misplace your hairbrush.

Labelling your feelings will also help you to share them with others. If a friend upsets you, you'll be able to explain how you feel and patch things up.

Look for Reasons to Laugh

The world has both good and bad in it. If you look for bad things, you will surely find them. But if you seek out the good things, the joyful things, you are sure to find them too.

So look for reasons to laugh. And chuckle your way through every single day.

Race-car drivers don't look at the pavement in front of their wheels. They look as far down the road as they can. Where your eyes look, your brain and body follow.

Keep Your Eye on the Prize

You've set a goal, like running your first 5k race. You're going to strap on those running shoes and follow a regular training schedule! But life has a way of interfering with goals. So how do you stay on track?

Simple: keep your eye on the prize. Put reminders of your goal wherever you will see them — on your desk, on the bathroom mirror, in your pocket. Set reminders on your phone.

Steel Yourself for Life's Challenges

Steel is a super-strong metal. It isn't found in nature. It starts out as iron ore, a very ordinary rock, then goes through a process of smelting, tempering and annealing to make it stronger and flexible.

You are like steel. The process that makes you stronger and helps you learn how to bend, not break, is called life. The more hardships and obstacles you overcome, the stronger you get.

So celebrate your challenges. They will make you steel-tough. They will make you shine.

Be Enthusiastic

Do you absolutely adore making miniatures? Or maybe you're mad about manga.

Enthusiasm is the foundation for success. When you throw yourself wholeheartedly into a subject, you are more likely to master it. You'll also have more fun!

Have a Goal

Do you dream of winning an Oscar? Owning your own multi-billion-dollar start-up? Or helping protect coral reefs?

If you have a dream, a goal, a fantasy that you're determined to make come true, good for you. It doesn't even matter if you ever achieve it. Simply having a goal and working toward it is tons of fun and makes every day a new adventure.

When you reach it, celebrate!

Then set a new goal, and begin working toward that!

Open Your Mind

Open your mind to . . .

- ★ New ideas
- ★ New experiences
- ★ New people

Learn from Everyone

Even a sage can learn from a fool.

Treat everyone you meet with respect.

You never know what they might teach you.

> "What separates the talented individual from the successful one is a lot of hard work."
>
> — Stephen King

Talent vs. Skill

You probably know kids who seem to have incredible talents. They're superb artists or great hockey players or super clever with words.

They are sooo talented, you think. *They're bound to succeed!*

Maybe. Maybe not. There's a huge difference between having an inborn talent and becoming successful. It's the application of time (lots of it!) and effort (even more!) that turns talent into skill.

If you're willing to work hard, you can take any degree of talent to the next level. So don't waste your energy comparing yourself to others. Instead, focus on developing your own unique abilities.

Talent + Hard Work = Mastery

Step by Step

When you dream of your glorious future, do you picture the road to your destination, or does the leap from HERE to THERE seem so huge that it makes the dream recede impossibly out of reach?

To avoid feeling overwhelmed, get in the habit of viewing your path to success as a series of small, easy-to-manage steps. You know you can do that first bit, right? Do it! When you've accomplished that step, focus only on the next teeny weeny one. Don't think about what comes afterwards.

Following this plan, you'll make steady progress without getting overwhelmed. Slowly, little by little, your goal will come closer.

During the course of a marathon, the average runner will take more than 40,000 steps.

Add Weight to Your Pros and Cons List

Making a tricky decision? Kick your pros and cons lists up to the next level and make better decisions by assigning a "weight," or a score, to each item on your list. This score will reflect how important the item is to you. For example, consider the list on the next page.

At first glance, the two columns seem closely matched. Of course they are — that's why it's such a tough decision to make! But when you weight each entry, you fine-tune the list for a more accurate read. In this case, the PRO side edges out the CON by five points.

Using a weighted pros and cons list, you now feel more confident in your decision. You go to the party and have a blast.

Going to Samsa's Birthday Party at the Bowling Alley!

PRO

I love parties!
- 70 points -

If I go, I won't get FOMO
- 5 points -

I will get to meet Samsa's other friends, and they sound awesome
- 10 points -

Total: 85 points

CON

I don't know how to bowl
- 20 points -

I have swim practice the next a.m. (tired!)
- 25 points -

I won't know anybody but Samsa - awkward!
- 35 points -

Total: 80 points

Delegate

You've got a project on the go. Say, a fundraiser for your local animal shelter. There's tons of work to do: making and hanging up posters, getting local businesses on board, and buying supplies for the big event. The clock is ticking, and you're nowhere near ready!

Letting go of parts of a project that's close to your heart can be hard. But you can't do it all. Take a tip from the CEOs of big corporations and delegate. Figure out which jobs are the ones only you can do (speaking to local businesses) and hand off other tasks (buying supplies and hanging posters) to your team.

Share the Credit

Yay you! You got a great grade, scored the winning goal, broke the school record. You have every reason to be proud of your success.

Go ahead and celebrate, but be sure to share the credit with the people who helped make it happen.

Giving shout-outs to your peeps doesn't diminish your victories. It makes them feel even sweeter, because it's way more fun to celebrate with others than on your own. Friends and teammates will also appreciate your generosity and thoughtfulness.

So when people congratulate you, make sure to highlight the contributions of those who helped you triumph. You'll be glad you did, and so will they!

Learn from the Duck

Yes, the world can seem downright weird at times. It can be frustrating too, especially when things don't go the way you think they should.

Don't let the little things get to you. Let them roll off you, like water off a duck's back.

Keep Paddling

You know how ducks look like they're floating along, calm and serene?

Under the water's surface, their webby feet are paddling furiously.

If you want to get ahead, keep calm and paddle on!

Avoid the Label Trap

You often hear people described with a label: math genius, athlete, rock star. Sometimes people even label themselves. The problem with labels is that they set limits and define expectations. They convey the message: "You are just this one thing."

But people are much more complicated and way more interesting!

Don't fall into the label trap. Think less about what people are, and more about what they do. Say, "He enjoys doing math" instead of, "He's a math genius." When you hear a label being used, fix it by adding the phrase, "among other things" at the end, and you'll see people more completely.

Be a Cat

Cats are resilient. Even when they fall from a great height, they land on their feet, then they spring right back into action.

So be like a cat. You might not always land on your feet. You might even take a few licks. That's okay! You're a CAT. And you're wonderful!

Give More Than You Get

Be a giver.

Share information. Share smiles and hugs. Give your time, or your money, to others who might need it more than you do.

That's when the magic happens. Because when you are generous with your knowledge, your heart, your time or your money, you get back more than you give away.

You win the love and admiration of others. You earn loyalty. You create a community that can help you out when you need it.

And you feel good inside.

It really is better to give than to receive.

Givers vs. Takers

Generosity is a wonderful trait. But it can
sometimes have a downside. Some people are
practised takers and will take advantage of your
good heart. Your gut will tell you who these
people are. Trust it, and be wise about who you
choose to give to.

Start Today

You've got a dream, and it's a big one! *One day*, you think, *I'll make it happen.*

Start taking steps toward making your dream a reality.

Read up on your favourite topic, and learn as much as you can about it now. Also find out which steps you will need to take to get from here to there.

By preparing now, you'll be ready to shoot out of the gate the moment the starting bell goes off.

Ask Around

Many people go to close friends or family for advice when they need to make a decision. That's a great technique. But it's only the start.

Kick your decision-making skills up a notch by also getting advice from people who are very different from you. Older people, younger people, people from different backgrounds — the more the merrier.

Why? Experts say that the ideas generated by people who resemble us tend to resemble our own ideas.

A wider, more diverse set of opinions from a wider, more diverse set of people usually yields more varied and creative ways of looking at a problem.

So ask around for advice! The results might surprise you and help you make top-notch decisions.

Find a Mentor

Mentors are like counsellors. They share what they know about a subject and give you good advice based on their experience. They can help speed you along your way to achieving your goals and advise you on how to avoid common pitfalls.

Where can you find a mentor? Teachers and librarians are good people to ask about how to make useful, safe contacts. For example, if you're interested in photography, they might be able to steer you to a club for photography enthusiasts in your area. They might even turn out to be great mentors themselves!

Be a Mentor

When you mentor others, you learn how to lead and encourage. You improve your ability to communicate clearly and kindly — skills that will benefit you in all areas of life.

Mentoring will also make you happy. You will undoubtedly experience the joy and pride that comes from watching your protege progress. Many people enjoy seeing someone they've mentored flourish even more than they enjoy achieving their own goals.

A mentorship doesn't have to be a formal relationship or a long-term one. Mentoring can mean helping a younger student master their ABCs or assisting a sibling in getting the hang of their new scooter.

Practise, Practise, Practise

Your brain is an active, ever-morphing organ. And that's thanks to what you put into it.

The brain is composed of billions of nerve cells, or neurons. Over time, the neurons form connections to each other. The more connections there are between groups of neurons, the more efficient and capable these groups become.

Whenever you learn a new skill, your brain builds a new set of connections. The more you practise that skill, the deeper and more numerous the connections become, taking you from a clumsy beginner to a smooth, powerful pro. That's why practice, and lots of it, is the surest way to success in any endeavour.

Give Yourself a Break

If you're working toward a goal but find yourself wanting to throw your hands in the air and shout, "I give up!" that means it's time for a break.

Even the most determined people don't work 24/7. Taking some time off to relax, to change gears, to try something new, helps you achieve your goals.

A time out lets you come back to a task refreshed and better able to complete it.

On a deadline? Make your break very short: a walk around the block, a quick doodle, a five-minute dance party.

Trust Your Natural Talent for Growth

You've just gotten the chance to try out speed skating or learn how to make funny cool origami frogs. You want to give it a go — *gulp!* — but you aren't sure you're up to the challenge.

Keep in mind that new experiences are like fertilizer; they help you grow. And growing is what kids do best! You're doing it right now, without even thinking about it.

The more new things you try, the stronger you will grow. And the better prepared you will be for whatever challenges life throws at you.

Advice from the Willow

Willow trees are soft. Their branches are flexible. When a storm hits, they bend, letting the gale toss their branches this way and that. They might lose some leaves, but in general, willows can withstand almost any onslaught.

Oak trees, on the other hand, are made of very hard wood. They do not bend. And while oaks can live a long time, in a huge storm, their limbs can get torn off. Seemingly invincible oaks might end up on the forest floor, totally uprooted.

When you find yourself in difficult times, learn from the willow. Not every situation should be faced head-on with dogged resistance.

You may find a willingness to bend is your greatest strength.

Get Back out There

When you fail at something — especially in a very public, or embarrassing way — it's natural to want to avoid doing that again. Avoidance is a way of protecting yourself from disappointment.

Instead, try to get right back out there. Chances are you won't have a repeat of your doomed performance. Instead, you will overwrite the unpleasant memory with a neutral or positive one. Your one-act tragedy will become the first part of a multipart drama in which you overcome obstacles and succeed.

If you fall off a horse and get back on, you might discover it's actually a unicorn.

Learn from the Eagle

When an eagle takes to the sky, it gets a whole new perspective. It enjoys a "bird's-eye view" — a wider and clearer outlook on what lies below. Obstacles that loomed large down on the ground shrink to near invisibility.

Even though you don't have wings, you too can learn to rise above the mundane and see the bigger picture. Make it a habit to take the long view. Like the mighty eagle, you will soar.

Get Comfy with Conflict

Maybe you've had a spat with a friend. Or perhaps you don't like the way your coach snapped at your team when you lost a big game.

Everyone, at some point or another, will find themselves in conflict with other people. Because conflict can often feel uncomfortable, it's natural for people to try to avoid dealing with it.

Understand Conflicts

Sometimes conflicts arise out of simple misunderstandings or miscommunication. For example, you think your friend didn't care about your feelings, when in reality she didn't know what your feelings were.

The first step, then, is to figure out what's going on. Share your feelings with the other party and listen to their point of view as well.

Next, try to restate each person's position in clear language: "So if I've got this right, you're annoyed that I used your coloured pencils without asking you for permission. And I'm upset because you crumpled up the picture I spent an hour creating."

Feeling heard can be a powerful step toward healing. Once you've shared your feelings, both you and the other person will probably start feeling much better.

Cool It!

When your emotions are stirred up, you are not able to think as clearly as when you are calm. That's why giving yourself — and the person you're at odds with — a cooling-off period is so useful.

Your cool-down might last a few minutes or a few days, depending on the situation. Give yourself the time you need.

Afterward you'll be more likely to come to a reasonable solution to the problem, one that satisfies everyone.

Avoid Making Conflicts Worse

Here are some golden rules to avoid turning a petty squabble into an all-out war:

★ No matter how angry you are, never attack the other person verbally or physically. If you feel like you can't control yourself, remove yourself from the situation.

★ Avoid yelling. Loud voices ramp up the tension without contributing anything new.

★ Stick to the topic. Don't bring up hurts from the past.

★ Use "I" statements, like, "I was hurt when I found out you were talking about me behind my back," rather than, "You were gossiping about me."

★ Leave room for the other person to "save face" and keep their pride intact. Even if you are totally in the right, making the other person feel ashamed or humiliated usually backfires. If they feel cornered, they might also feel they have no other choice but to lash out.

Brainstorm Solutions to Conflicts

Once you have clearly established what a conflict is about, and both of you are calm and able to talk to each other respectfully, you are in the best position to come up with a resolution that will satisfy both of you. This is the time to brainstorm some solutions.

Your brainstorming session might result in one of these solutions:

★ An apology. If you did something wrong or hurtful, intentionally or unintentionally, say you're sorry.

★ Restitution. If you lost or damaged something that belongs to someone else, repair or replace it.

★ A plan. Come up with a strategy for facing a similar situation in the future.

Agree on a Solution

The ultimate goal in conflict resolution is coming up with a solution. Ideally it will be a "win-win," where both of you are satisfied with the outcome. If you can't agree on the solution, you might consider bringing in a third person whom you both trust to help you find common ground.

Once you have reached an agreement, honour your part of it. If you've promised to do something, do it. Give the other person a chance to do what they've promised to do too.

Don't forget to check in with the other person in a few hours or a few days. Make sure that they are okay with your agreement and that they feel ready to move on.

Know When to Move On

Not every conflict will end in a resolution that is satisfying to everyone. And some people can't get over hurt feelings no matter what you do. It's unfortunate when this happens, but you don't have to let it get to you.

Remember: time will pass, and whatever situation you find yourself in will change.

You can't change other people's feelings and you aren't responsible for them. If you've made a sincere effort to solve the problem, and the other person will not meet you halfway, then it's their problem, not yours.

Know when it's time to move on, and do it.

Once is a mistake.
Twice is a pattern.
Three times is a habit.

Once Is a Mistake . . .

Uh oh! You've messed up. Badly. And now you want to sink into the floor and pretend it never happened. Don't do it! You'll feel better faster if you don't go into avoidance mode.

Accidents don't happen in a vacuum. Something occurred beforehand that made that boo-boo possible. Take a few moments to figure out what it was. Then ask yourself, "Is there something I can do so I don't make that same mistake again?" For example, if you spilled apple juice all over your just-finished homework, in the future you can make sure not to leave the glass where it could be easily knocked over.

Taking a closer look at what happened will help protect you from making similar mistakes in the future. By taking concrete action now, you also gain a feeling of control over the future, which will make you feel better now!

Cross-Train

You know that exercise is good for both your body and your soul. But what kind of exercise is best?

All of it. Your body needs variety. Some activities build strength, others build endurance or flexibility. So to be your best physical self, cross-train. That means do different sports and physical activities.

If you're a soccer player, practising nothing but soccer day in and day out won't get you to the top of your field. Try other complementary activities — such as yoga, swimming or tai chi — that improve flexibility, strength and balance, which will help build endurance and prevent injury.

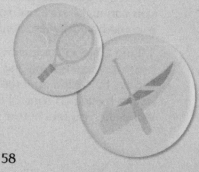

Vary the Intensity

Top athletes know they can't go all out all the time. They need to rest muscles between hard training sessions and vary the intensity of their training.

That's why marathon runners, for example, alternate between different types of running workouts. One day might be a series of super-fast sprints. Another day would feature an easy, shorter run. A third might be the long-run day, going slowly and steadily for a distance. And one day might be reserved for a full twenty-four hours of rest and relaxation.

Whatever your sport, varying the intensity of your workouts will help you reach your goal faster and with less risk of injury.

Varying intensity works for many different life challenges, not just sports. Are you studying for a big test? Drawing a comic book or graphic novel? Learning a new piano piece? Break up your work schedule into light, medium and full intensity sessions. Remember to leave time for rest and relaxation too!

The Best Kind of Manners

Good manners aren't about knowing which fork to use. They're about kindness and being considerate of the people around you.

Having good manners is easy. You simply follow the golden rule: "Treat others the way you would like to be treated."

Manners Matter

Ramp up your good manners to great manners.

★ Be aware of what's going on around you. Are the people standing around the gym door waiting to get in? Don't cut ahead of them; wait your turn. Is someone standing near your table, lunch in hand, scanning the lunchroom for a seat? Shuffle over and make room for them.

★ Put yourself in other people's shoes. If you're having lunch with a friend, think about what they are seeing when they look at you. Do you want to see food in someone's mouth while they are chewing? They probably don't either. So keep your mouth closed.

★ Be respectful of others, especially in public places. That means cleaning up after yourself, keeping to one side of the aisle or sidewalk instead of striding down the middle, and avoiding loud conversations where you might be disturbing others.

Shift Your Focus

When you're waiting . . . and waiting . . . and waiting and that clock won't move any faster, shift your focus.

Take your eyes off that clock and think about something else for a few minutes — like that exciting book you've been reading! You might wish your waiting period never ends!

This also works for reducing physical pain. Stubbed your toe? Consciously shift your mental focus away from that throbbing foot to the tip of your nose, for example. The sore toe will not hurt quite as much!

Make It a Win-Win

Hockey, football, curling — in games like these, there is only one winner (+ 1), and one loser (- 1). These sorts of games are also called zero-sum games. They get that name because the two halves of the equation, when added together, equal zero: - 1 + 1 = 0.

Life doesn't have to be a zero-sum game. Another kind of game is called a "win-win." In those games, people work together to achieve a goal, and everybody comes out on top.

Look for ways to create win-win situations wherever you can. For example, after the next snowfall, get the neighbourhood kids all working together to build hilarious snow creatures instead of having a snowball fight.

Now that's a real win(ter)-win(ter)!

Go for Bronze?

Which would you be happier winning, a silver or a bronze medal? Most people think winning silver would be better. But according to one study, bronze medallists tend to be happier than their silver-winning peers. Why? The answer might lie in how they view the experience.

Silver medallists tend to focus on their failure; they weren't good enough to win. But bronze medallists tend to focus on the fact that they made it to the podium; they are thrilled to be there and get a medal. Isn't a bronze medal better than no medal at all? Even though they came in third, they feel like a winner!

So get in the habit of seeing your life through the eyes of a bronze medallist. You're here, on the podium of life! And you're doing great!

The Power of Three

Your mind, body and heart are the three powerful ingredients that make you you. All three parts work together and depend on each other. When the three are in harmony, you feel great. When they're not, you start to feel out of sorts.

To consistently feel your best:

★ Take care of your body by regularly giving it nutritious food, rest and exercise.

★ Take care of your mind by regularly feeding it with plenty of mental stimulation — books, music, puzzles, etc.

★ Take care of your heart by regularly spending time with friends and family and engaging in creative activities.

See the Forest AND the Trees

Have you ever heard the expression, "You can't see the forest for the trees?" This saying refers to not being able to see the big picture because you're too caught up in the little details.

Whether you're the kind of person who tends to see the forest, or one who tends to see the trees, you'll benefit from occasionally shifting your perspective. Whenever you start a project, take a moment to consider the big picture — what you aim to achieve. Also, jot down some concrete steps — the details to help you get there. This technique will get you in the habit of seeing both the forest *and* the trees.

Flow is a form
of play.

Get in the Zone

Some people call it "the zone." Some people call it "flow." Whatever you call it, the state of being so totally focused on an activity that the world slips away and time passes without you being aware of it feels great.

So how do you get into the zone?

1. Set aside time for your activity. Getting into flow takes preparation. Work that prep into your schedule.

2. Focus on your task. Clear your mind of everything else.

3. Remove distractions. Close the door, turn off your phone or any screens, and ask not to be interrupted while you are engaged in your task.

4. Dive in. Put aside any doubts or judgment about what you are doing. Flow is all about process, not results. The deeper you let yourself engage, the better the experience will be.

> "Success is liking yourself, liking what you do, and liking how you do it."
>
> — Maya Angelou

What Is Success?

Success means different things to different people. For some it might mean having a fancy job and driving a flashy car. To others, success might mean composing an uplifting symphony or living a life of service.

Only you can decide what matters most to you. You get to set both the goal and where the goalposts stand.

Nobody's Perfect

It's not always pleasant to think about our flaws, but if you can find the courage to look at yourself honestly, you will have found a powerful tool for crafting success.

By confronting your weaknesses, you give yourself a chance to figure out how to overcome them. You can even take practical steps to eliminate them. If you admit you really don't have a firm handle on the seven times tables, you can practise.

Another benefit of acknowledging your limits is that you'll feel more comfortable asking for help. Collaborating with others might become your best strategy.

Celebrate Your Strengths

Yes, we all have weaknesses. But we also have strengths.

Whatever unique abilities you have, it's important to acknowledge them. If you only focus on your weaknesses, you can easily wind up feeling bad about yourself. You might also make poor decisions because you're not drawing upon all the facts!

That's why self-knowledge — having an accurate sense of both your strengths and weaknesses — is such a valuable trait. It keeps you pointing toward your dreams while showing you what you need to do to get there.

Embrace Change

Change can be scary. It brings with it uncertainty and challenges you might feel unprepared to face.

But change also brings opportunity.

You can't prevent change from occurring, but you can control how you react to it. Embrace it!

Listen to Your Gut

Do you ever get a niggling sensation that you know something without being able to pinpoint how? Some people call it intuition. Others call it having a hunch or a gut feeling. No matter what you call it, listen to it.

If your body reacts strongly to a situation, pay attention. Your mind works so quickly, messages can sometimes get to your gut faster than they can to the decision-making part of your brain.

You might feel a strange tightening in your belly that signals danger. Or you might feel a little flutter of joy.

Either way, trust your gut.

Take Baby Steps

You didn't learn to walk all in one go.

Runners don't reach the finish line by taking a single giant step either.

You get where you want to go when you put one foot in front of the other every day. You may have to take hundreds of baby steps to see any progress, but if you keep walking, sooner or later you will get there.

> "A journey of a thousand miles begins with a single step."
>
> — Lao Tzu

Find Your Stride

The hardest part of any journey is the moment before you begin. That's when the task ahead can seem so daunting, so overwhelming, you want to give up.

But it's when you take that first step that the magic happens. You find your stride. You start to enjoy the journey. What looked like mountains turn out to be nothing but bumps in the road.

You've got this!

So take a deep breath and take that first step.

Attitude Adjustment

It's inevitable — sooner or later, life is going to throw you a curve ball. You will face disappointment and loss.

At those times, you can blame yourself (or other people) for things that aren't your fault (or theirs) and claim that "life isn't fair." Or you can take life's knocks in stride and realize that the universe isn't really out to get you. With time and effort you can recover. You can even grow and become stronger and more resilient thanks to the challenges life throws at you.

Remember: Tomorrow is another day. Greet it with joy!

Quit the Blame Game

Take responsibility for your actions and accept the consequences.

CAUTION:
Road Block

Give yourself permission to succeed. Many of us don't. We put roadblocks in our way. We set up situations for ourselves that make it harder to succeed than it should be. Some of these roadblocks are obvious, like "forgetting" to study for the big test. Others are mental habits, like negative self-talk ("I'm not smart enough"), that consistently trip us up.

Kick roadblocks aside! See how much easier your path will be if you do.

Start by tackling these common roadblocks:

★ Negative thinking. Focus on the positive steps required to move ahead.

★ Procrastination. Get cracking!

★ Quitting at the first obstacle. Recognize that bumps in the road will happen, but you have the tools to climb over them. Stick with it until you do.

Focus on Finishing

Do you have a secret stash of unfinished projects in your closet? Maybe a scarf you started to knit and never completed or an amazing model spaceship you only got partway through?

Some people would rather quit than be disappointed with the end result. But seeing things through brings rewards beyond the finished product.

Most big projects, especially ones that rely on skills that are new to you, don't come out A1 the first time. But every time you complete a project, you learn from your mistakes, guaranteeing that it will come out better next time. And when you focus on finishing, you're developing your ability to persevere, which will help you face tough challenges in the future.

Silly, Sillier, Silliest!

Let's be serious for a moment. It isn't silly to let yourself go on occasion; it's smart. It can change your perspective and your mood. It can help you blow off steam.

So pull the goofy face. Do the kooky dance step. Tell the dumb joke.

It's seriously fun.

Give It a Go!

The only real failure is refusing to try.

Find Your People

Your people are those who share a certain worldview. With them you won't be the only one who's nuts about narwhals, has a passion for pancakes or is mad about math.

No matter how quirky or offbeat you are, there are people out there who share your interests, attitudes and enthusiasm. Find them.

Make a Great First Impression

Meeting new people and making new friends is one of life's greatest joys. So naturally you'll want to put your best foot forward! Here's how:

★ Stand up straight. Slouching or slumping sends the message you lack confidence.

★ Good grooming is important. Make sure your hair, face and hands are clean and tidy.

★ Make eye contact.

★ Introduce yourself. Speak clearly and loudly enough to be easily heard.

★ If the situation calls for it (like meeting your mom's boss), offer a handshake.

★ Smile. Who can resist your charming grin?

That's it! Now it's the other person's turn to impress you!

Four Steps to Success

When you're faced with a — gulp — seriously nerve-wracking challenge, like starring in a school play or trying your first double flip on a trampoline, put this simple four-step plan to work. It builds confidence while taking the edge off anxiety.

1. Set a goal. Focus on the short term. If emotions threaten to get in the way, count out loud or think about the reasons why you're doing what you're doing.

2. Visualize. Picture yourself doing the task at hand and succeeding. Practising the steps mentally prepares your mind and body to do them in real life.

3. Give yourself a pep talk. Repeat positive phrases out loud or in your head: "You can do this. You got this. You're well prepared." The steady stream of positive self-talk forces out both doubt and fear.

4. Breathe. Take deep, slow and steady breaths to calm your mind and give yourself time to think through your plan.

Give up Unrealistic Expectations

So you want to be a pop star. Before you turn twenty-one. Okay, then . . .

Everyone needs a dream. But there's a difference between a dream and an unrealistic expectation.

An unrealistic expectation is a dream that you expect to come true in a magical sort of way. Like you'll jot down a song and poof! The next thing you know you're an internet sensation. That's not impossible, but it's not likely either. Most people need to work long and hard for their dreams to come true.

Instead, take a good hard look at your expectations. Make sure you develop an achievable plan that will lead you toward it one step at a time.

Hope for the Best

Imagining possible future obstacles can sometimes become an excuse for not trying anything new.

Fearing that the cake might burn isn't a reason to skip getting out the mixer though. Your strawberry shortcake might indeed turn out wonky. But then again, it might turn out A1!

So prepare for the obstacles, but also hope for the best.

Plan for the Worst

It's your big sister's birthday and you've decided to make her a birthday cake. BEFORE you get out the mixing bowls, take a few minutes to imagine a very sad cake and an equally sad Future You.

Maybe Future You is looking at a Bundt that's burnt to a crisp. Or maybe there's more buttercream in your hair than on the cake!

Once you've identified potential pitfalls, you can avoid them. For example, when Today You goes to bake that cake, you'll make sure to use an oven timer and to wait to ice it until it's completely cooled. Your sister's birthday cake will be picture perfect — and scrumptious too.

Perfect vs. Good Enough

Sorry to be the one to tell you, but you're not perfect. No one is. And it's unlikely you will ever have the perfect game, the perfect school record or the perfect model airplane collection.

That's a good thing.

Once you realize and accept that perfection is impossible, you are free — free of false expectations, free to fail, free to be yourself.

You can never achieve perfection, but you can keep striving to become the best you can be.

Be a Rhino

Rhinos have notoriously tough hides that help protect them from injury.

Having "thick skin" — the ability to withstand harsh words or criticism — can protect you from hurt too.

Not everyone is born with thick skin, but growing some isn't hard! If you feel slighted or hurt, take a step back and ask yourself, "What's this really about?" instead of automatically assuming it's about you. Recognize that when a person says something mean, it says more about them than about you.

A hurtful comment can sting, but in the long-run, how much will it matter? You're a rhino! With your thick hide, you barely even feel those pesky gnat bites!

Reflect

When you have a lot on the go, you can find yourself feeling like you're spinning out of control.

Giving yourself quiet time to reflect on your day, your feelings or your plans helps defeat that spinny feeling. A few minutes of "me time," during which you take stock and let your mind and body settle down, will help you feel calmer, more grounded and more in control.

Put "quiet reflection" on your calendar. Schedule it in every morning before you leave for school or just before bed.

Make your sense of well-being a priority.

My motto is . . .
have a motto.

Choose Words to Live By

A motto is a phrase or saying that sums up your overall philosophy. It helps motivate you and keeps you focused on what is most important to you.

Choosing your own motto is a simple yet powerful way to help you achieve your dreams.

★ It can be something you borrow from someone else or something you write yourself.

★ It can be funny: "Life is uncertain; eat dessert first!"

★ It can be short and sweet: "Always do your best."

You don't have to share your motto with anyone else. And you can change it any time.

Whatever you choose, make your motto work for you.

Talk Yourself Through It

You got a birdhouse kit for your birthday and you're excited to build a happy home for Mr. and Mrs. Robin. You're nervous too. What if you mess up the birdhouse?

Quell those nerves by talking yourself through the task out loud.

★ Ask yourself "What am I missing?" to see the problem more clearly.

★ Tell yourself "I can try several ways to make this work" to stay on track.

★ Getting frustrated? Say, "I need a ten-minute breather." Then make a plan for when you'll return to the task.

By talking yourself through your project, you become your own pep squad. Eventually, you won't need to say the words out loud. They'll become part of you.

Half Empty or Half Full?

Are you the sort that sees a cup as half empty or half full?

It's both and it's neither. The cup is life. It's waiting to be filled by you.

Start pouring, and fill your cup with so much joy it overflows.

Appreciate the Little Things

Relish life's small, everyday joys.

A cool drink of water when you're thirsty. The way crisp white snow blazes bright pink at sunset. The soft touch of your stuffed bunny as you snuggle up in bed.

These sparkling moments are yours and yours alone. No one can take them away from you. No one can diminish them.

Cherish them, and enjoy them to the fullest.

Envision It

Great athletes spend hours and hours practising — in their heads. They picture themselves hitting a ball or making a stunning swan dive perfectly over and over again.

While it doesn't replace actual physical practice, mental practice (visualization) definitely helps. Your brain–body connections are strengthened each time you picture yourself succeeding at a task. So the next time you try that task in the real world, you're better at it than the last time.

Visualization works for skills other than sports too. Playing a musical instrument, giving a speech, or mastering a tricky dance step can all get a boost from mental rehearsal.

The Power of Zzzzzzzzz

Most kids need at least eight hours of sleep each night. Some may need a lot more. If you're dragging yourself through the day, you might not be getting enough.

These tips might help:

- ★ Try going to bed earlier.

- ★ Go to bed and wake up at roughly the same times every day.

- ★ Keep your bedroom dark and quiet.

- ★ Avoid screens right before bed. They interfere with quality sleep.

- ★ Have a warm bath or shower before bed to help you drift off faster.

Memorize It!

Why bother memorizing things when our digital devices store so much information right at our fingertips? There are a few reasons:

★ Memorization strengthens your brain and makes it easier for you to learn.

★ Memorizing a longish piece of text — like your favourite song — gives you a sense of achievement.

★ When you memorize something, you can call it up effortlessly when you need it. Try it with your multiplication tables. When you know them by heart, you'll whiz through complicated mathematical problems that rely on these math basics.

You're in Charge of HMCS YOU

Who's captain of your personal ship?

You are.

Keep your hand on the wheel, your eye on the horizon, and steer your ship to success.

Walk Tall

Do you meet the world with your head held high?

Walking tall is a simple way to boost your mood. Lifting your chest gives your lungs more room and lets them take in more oxygen. That makes you feel more energized. Throwing back your shoulders instead of letting them hunch forward will also help you feel more relaxed and confident.

Not sure if you're walking tall? Imagine a balloon is tied to the top of your head and lifting up, up, up!

Doesn't that feel good?

Watch Your Language

We've all heard, "Sticks and stones can break my bones, but words can never hurt me."

Not true. Words are powerful and can cause plenty of harm. Choose your words carefully. Think before you speak and consider the following:

★ Is what I'm about to say true?

★ Is it hurtful?

★ Will I offend or confuse someone?

★ What do I hope to achieve by saying this?

Pay attention to the words you say inside your head too. Are they mostly negative or positive? Do they support your dreams and goals?

If you are careful in your language, your words will become a powerful force for good.

Are You Dreaming?

Some people have a dream. Others have a goal. What's the difference?

Commitment.

A goal involves a plan. If you stick to it, you'll transform your dream into reality.

Bounce!

You're a ball. Like a ball, you can soar into the air. Look! You're flying!

Like a ball, you might sometimes crash back to earth. And when you do, you'll bounce.

When life gets you down or hands you a disappointment, give yourself some time to recover. Then dust yourself off and get back out there. Before you know it, you'll be flying high again.

Take a Risk

DARE TO BE YOURSELF!

Cut Yourself
Some Slack

You've dropped your homework in the snow.
Argh! Don't beat yourself up about it.

Instead, imagine it was your friend who dropped
that homework in the snow. What would
you say to them? The same things you say to
yourself? Or would your words be kinder?

You'd probably tell them it wasn't that big a deal;
it could happen to anyone.

Do the same, then, for yourself. Cut yourself
some slack.